Mr. Plemmons,

Thank you for nurturing and supporting a love of reading and writing in our daughter Lauren. We are so grateful for all you have done for her as a teacher and mentor. Barrow has been a tremendous experience for all of us, and we are so thankful for your guidance.

Lisa Jost and Doug Haines

THE
NEW YORKER
BOOK OF TEACHER CARTOONS
REVISED AND UPDATED

THE NEW YORKER
BOOK OF TEACHER CARTOONS
REVISED AND UPDATED

EDITED BY ROBERT MANKOFF

INTRODUCTION BY LEE LORENZ

WILEY

John Wiley & Sons, Inc.

Published by John Wiley & Sons, Inc., Hoboken, New Jersey.
Published simultaneously in Canada.

For general information on our other products and services or for technical support, please contact our
Customer Care Department within the United States at (800) 762-2974, outside the United States at
(317) 572-3993 or fax (317) 572-4002.

Wiley also publishes its books in a variety of electronic formats. Some content that appears in print may
not be available in electronic books. For more information about Wiley products, visit our web site at
www.wiley.com.

Library of Congress Cataloging-in-Publication Data:

ISBN 978-1-118-34203-9 (cloth); ISBN 978-1-118-36232-7 (ebk);
ISBN 978-1-118-36233-4 (ebk); ISBN 978-1-118-36235-8 (ebk)

Printed in the United States of America

10 9 8 7 6 5

THE

NEW YORKER
BOOK OF TEACHER CARTOONS
REVISED AND UPDATED

BY LEE LORENZ

INTRODUCTION

The lengthening shadows of early autumn evoke a profound sense of unease. Dropping temperatures? Frozen pipes? The first snowfall? The achin' back?

No. Something deeper. Something primal!

THE FIRST DAY OF SCHOOL

It all comes back in a rush: The smell of chalk, the soggy peanut-butter-and-jelly sandwiches, the class brain, the schoolyard bully, staying after, homework.

THE REPORT CARD

We all share the recurring nightmares: The class we forgot to attend. The homework we _____. The locker combination we just plain forgot.

On the following pages, America's finest cartoonists revisit these intimate years, if not in tranquility at least without bitterness.

Barbara Smaller: One tot to another: "It's all learning-is-fun and invented spelling, then—bam!—second grade."

Liza Donnelly: "What I Did on My Summer Vacation: The Treatment."

Emily Flake: "It wasn't our first choice of schools, but we had a Groupon for it, so what the hell."

And the very hip William Haefeli: "Will Kristen, Kirsten, and Kiersten please choose new names?"

Read and enjoy.

There will be no written test afterward.

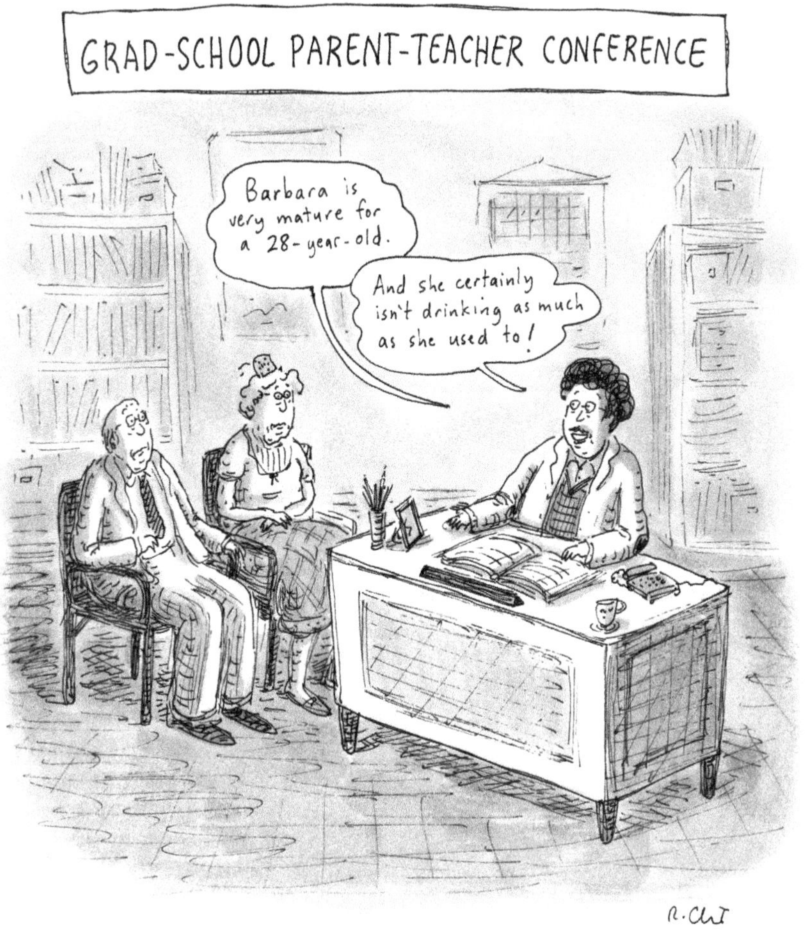
GRAD-SCHOOL PARENT-TEACHER CONFERENCE
Barbara is very mature for a 28-year-old.
And she certainly isn't drinking as much as she used to!
R. Cht

2nd PERIOD OPEN-MIKE PHYSICS

"Look, I know this stuff. But all these questions are
having a chilling effect."

"I need you to line up by attention span."

"Back in my day, kids had a little respect for the law of gravity."

"*There—now I've taught you everything I know about splitting rocks.*"

"What I Did on My Summer Vacation: The Treatment."

"Who knows the words to the theme song of the United States?"

"I'm holding George back this year because he's failed to forge a personal style."

"Rosalie—your poor performance this year has reduced your parents' investment in you by almost seventy per cent."

"Some hacker from an obscure university in China ate my homework."

"It's a great school, but it wasn't my first choice."

"It's all learning-is-fun and invented spelling,
then—bam!—second grade."

"We believe in the <u>concept</u> of public education."

"My parents didn't do my homework for me,
but I did bring them in as consultants."

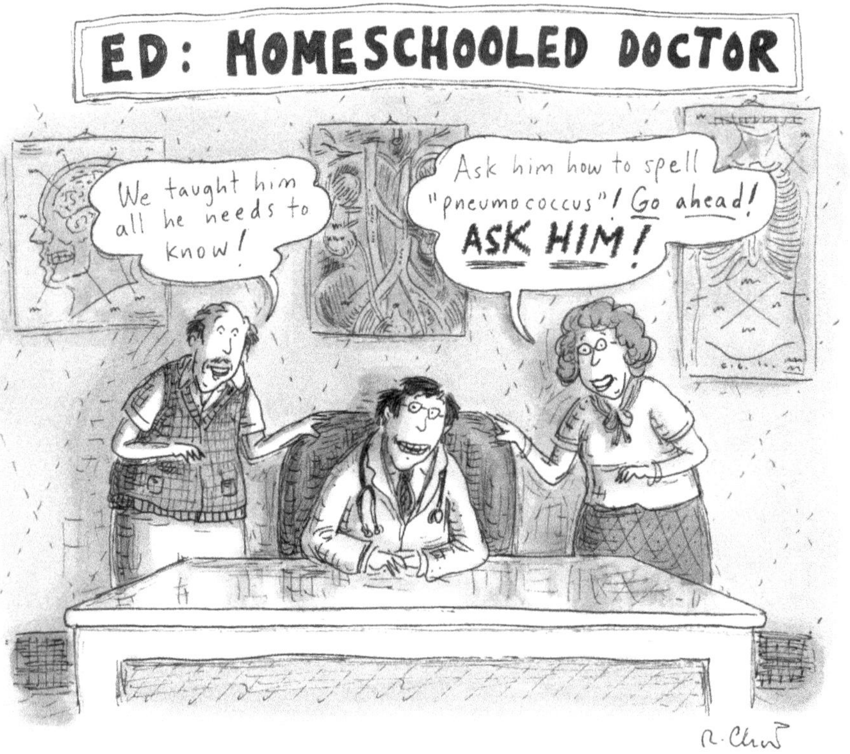
ED: HOMESCHOOLED DOCTOR
We taught him all he needs to know!
Ask him how to spell "pneumococcus"! Go ahead! ASK HIM!
R. Chast

"I swore I wouldn't make the same mistakes with
my children as my parents did with me."

"I have two mommies. I know where the apostrophe goes."

"Four 'Greats,' one 'Super-Duper,' and
a 'Special.' What's with the 'Special?'"

"It's a shame that she could never put
her college degree to use."

"Will Kristen, Kirsten, and Kiersten please choose new names?"

"Anyone following me on Twitter already knows what I did this past summer."

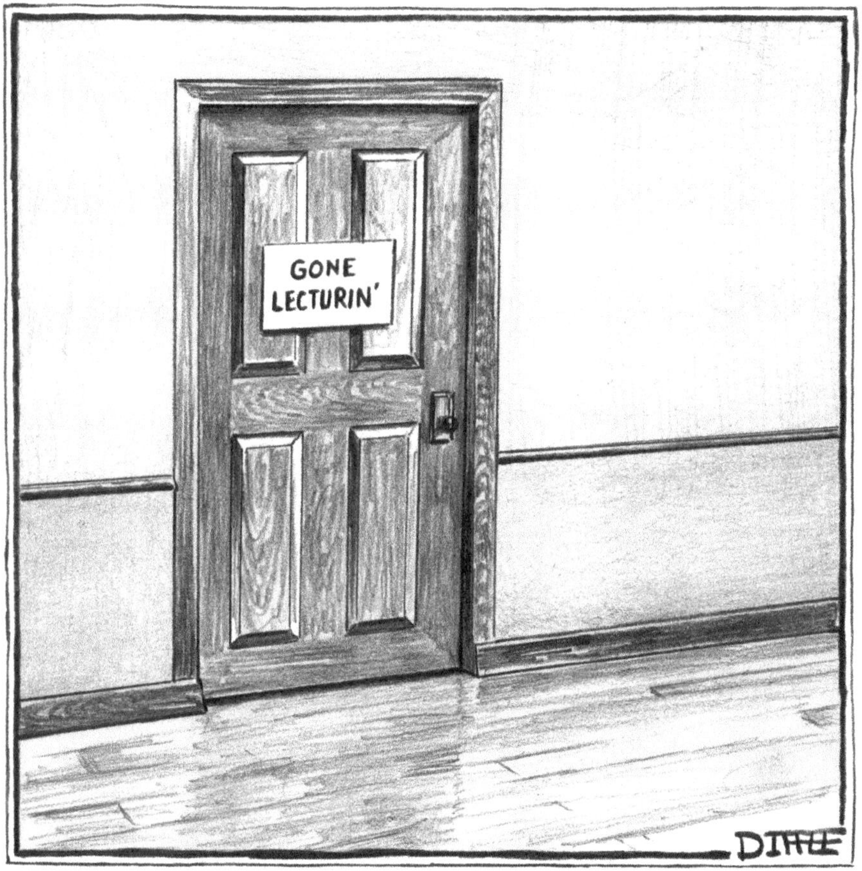
GONE
LECTURIN'
DIFFEE

"It wasn't our first choice of schools, but we had
a Groupon for it, so what the hell."

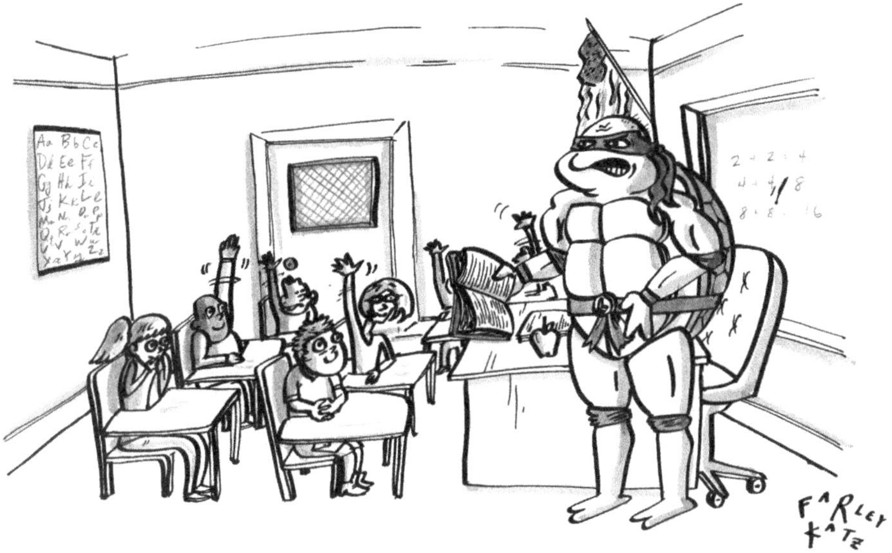
FARLEY KATZ

"O.K., I'll explain it one more time. Sometimes even very successful careers come to an end, and you have to teach the things you were once paid to do in order to make rent."

"Mrs. Hammond! I'd know you anywhere from
little Billy's portrait of you."

"'GameBoy: A Memoir of Addiction,' by Ronald Markowitz."

THE BERLITZ GUIDE TO PARENT - TEACHER CONFERENCES

TEACHERESE	ENGLISH
Marches to a different drummer.	Nuts.
Needs to brush up on his people skills.	Homicidal.
Creative.	None too bright
Very creative.	A moron, actually.
She's a riot!	I can't stand her.
He's doing just fine.	What's your kid's name again?

R. Chast

"Please, Ms. Sweeney, may I ask where you're going with all this?"

"*Where do you get off saying my kid is grade level?*"

THE FIRST DAY BACK

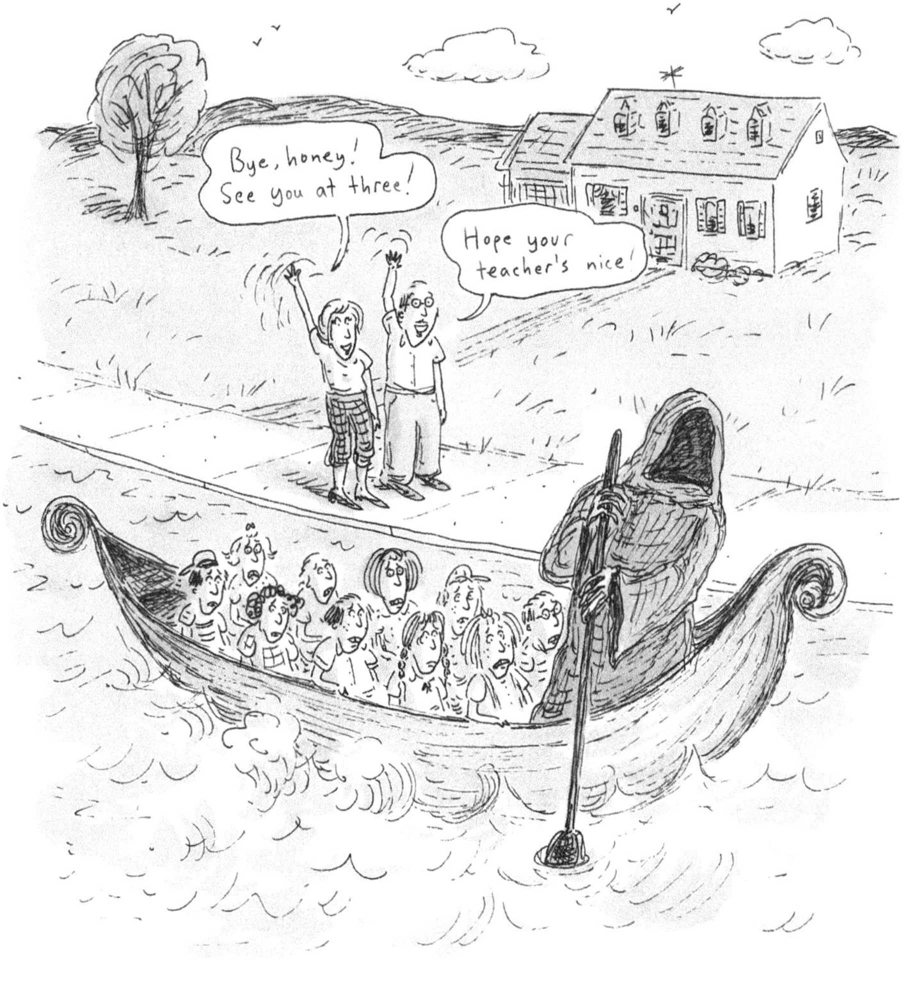
Bye, honey! See you at three!
Hope your teacher's nice!

"So, what are we aiming for, Timmy—the Nobel Prize or 'Inspected by No. 7'?"

"Mrs. Minton, there's no such thing as a bad boy. Hostile, perhaps. Aggressive, recalcitrant, destructive, even sadistic. But not <u>bad</u>."

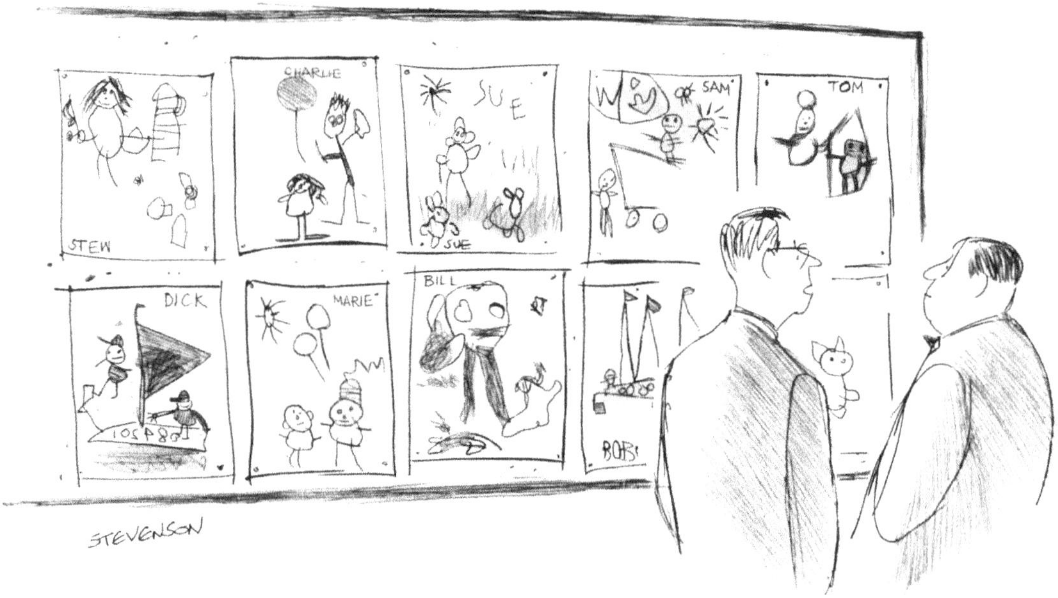
STEW
CHARLIE
SUE
SUE
SAM
TOM
DICK
MARIE
BILL
STEVENSON

"Which is yours?"

"No one's last words were 'I wish I'd done more homework.'"

"*Unfortunately, all evidence of your son's intelligence is purely anecdotal.*"

"This is Henderson, speaking for Miss Gordy's second-grade ad-hoc students' committee. Here's a list of our demands."

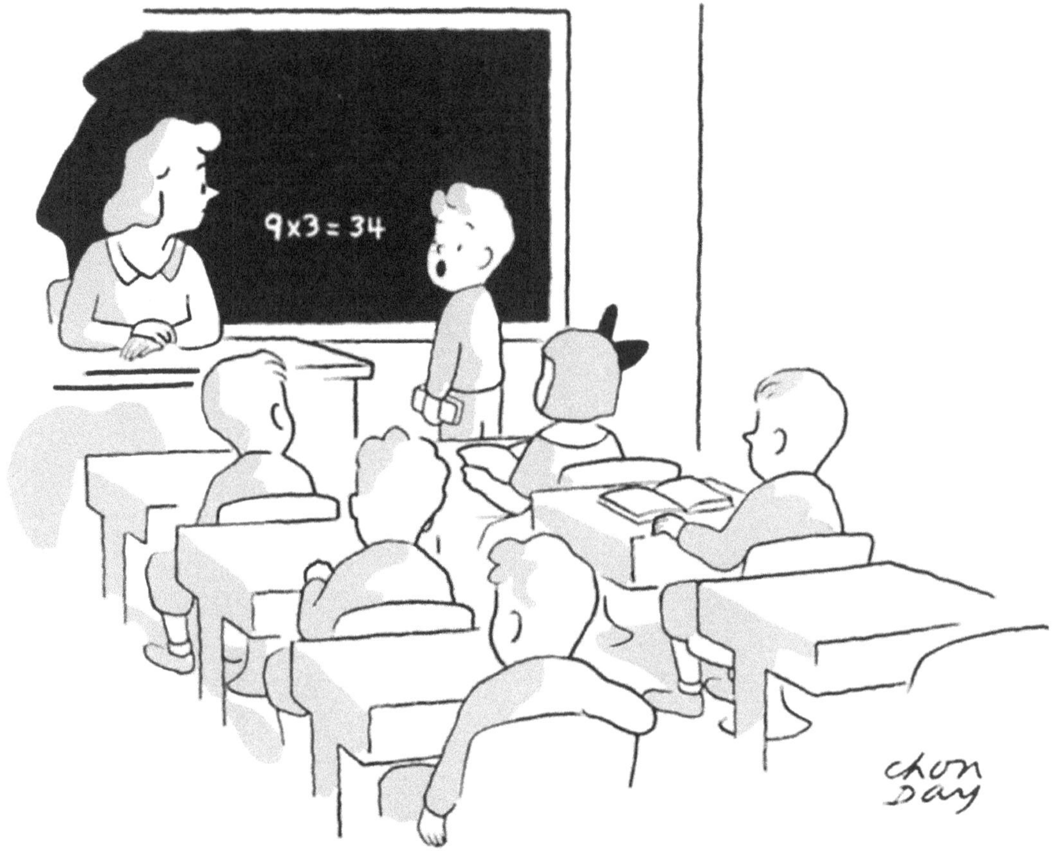
9x3 = 34
CHON DAY

"Am I warm?"

"My parents didn't write it—they just tweaked it."

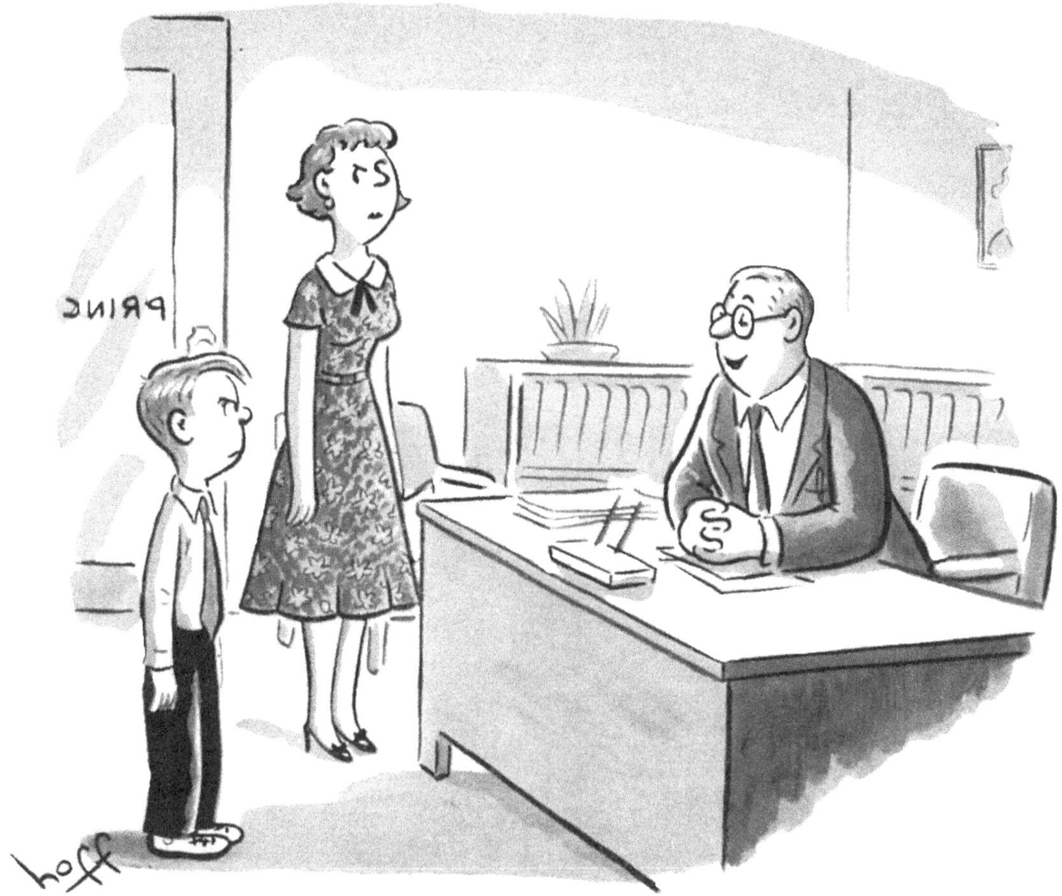
hoff

"Thompson, how about you and Miss Hobson shaking hands, and let's see if we can't make a fresh start."

"May I remind you, Jensen, that teacher evaluation by
the group has yet to be approved."

"I see trouble with algebra."

"In a nutshell, Mrs. Turner, either your son is making an unusually fine adjustment to his lack of ability or else he just doesn't give a damn."

"Your armies have deserted you, you have been wounded unto death. Now make me feel it!"

"But, Eugene, it's not enough to be gifted. We've got to *do* something with our gift."

"Miss Peterson, may I go home? I can't assimilate any more data today."

"I'm sorry, Timmy, but you are wrong. You are terribly, terribly wrong."

"We've created a safe, nonjudgemental environment that will leave your child ill-prepared for real-life."

"So *what* if the Applebaum kid thinks you're a down trip? The rest of your students gave you terrific report cards."

"*Thank you for coming. The talks were forthright and useful, and provided an excellent climate in which to resolve our remaining differences.*"

"Oh no, not homework again."

"So what if he paid a classmate to do
his homework—it was his own allowance."

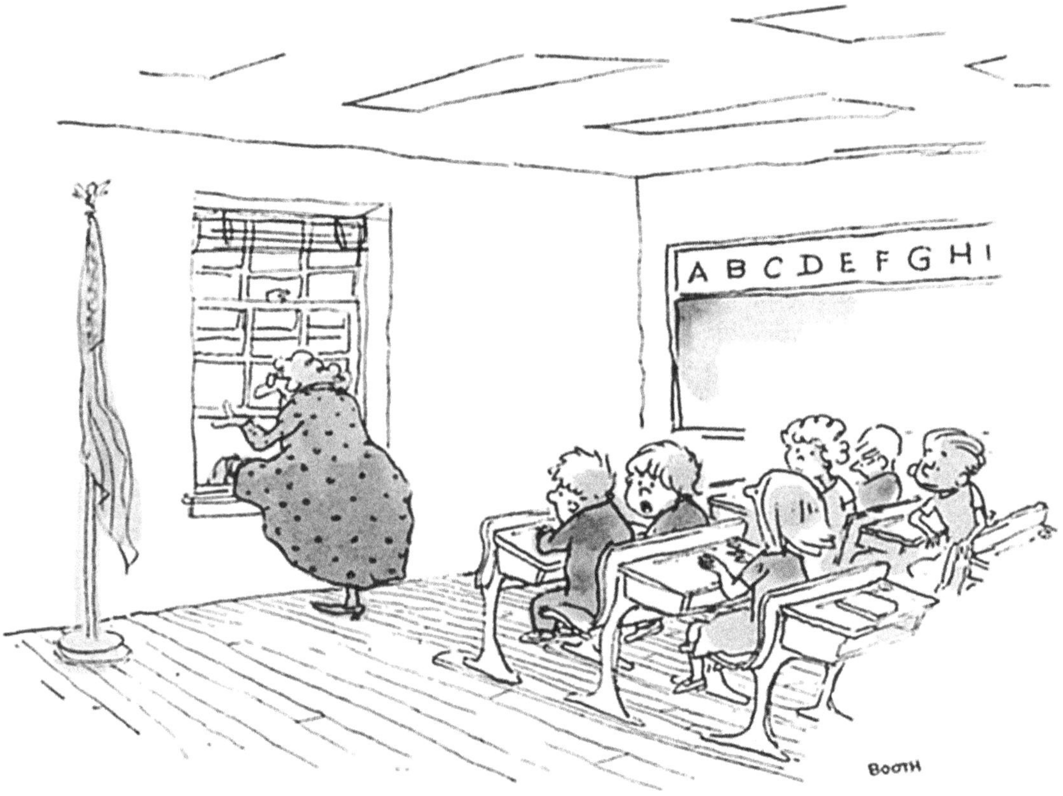
A B C D E F G H I
BOOTH

"Teacher burnout."

"All right, children, who wants to open our discussion of the Papa Bear's sense of rage? Tommy?"

"'What I Did on My Summer Vacation,' by special arrangement with the New Jersey State Police."

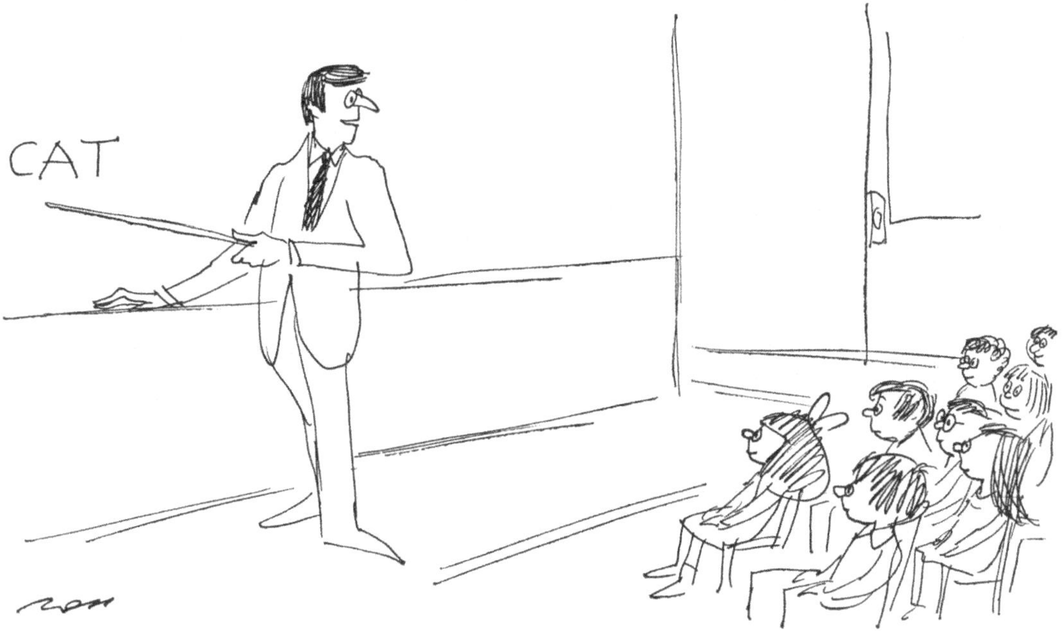
CAT

"To sum up . . ."

"He's very quick with an answer. But it's never the right one."

THE END OF INNOCENCE

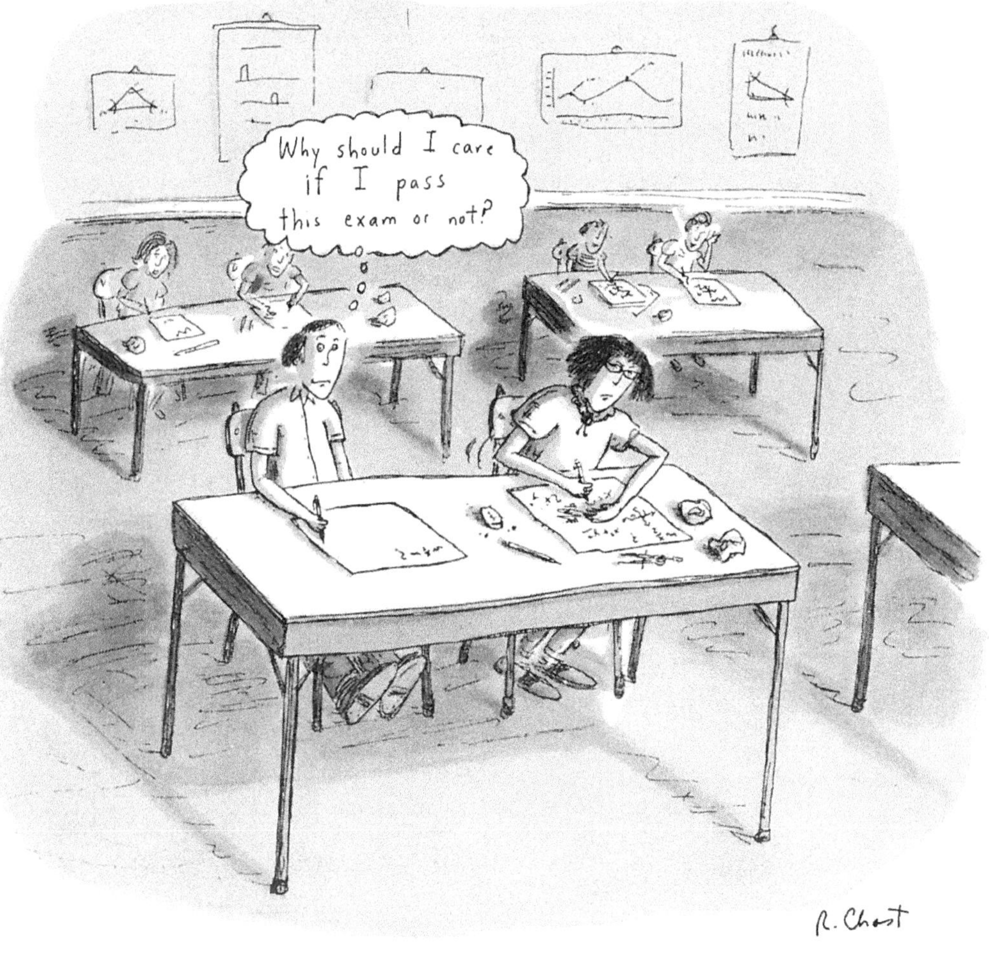
Why should I care if I pass this exam or not?
R. Chast

"That is the correct answer, Billy, but I'm afraid
you don't win anything for it."

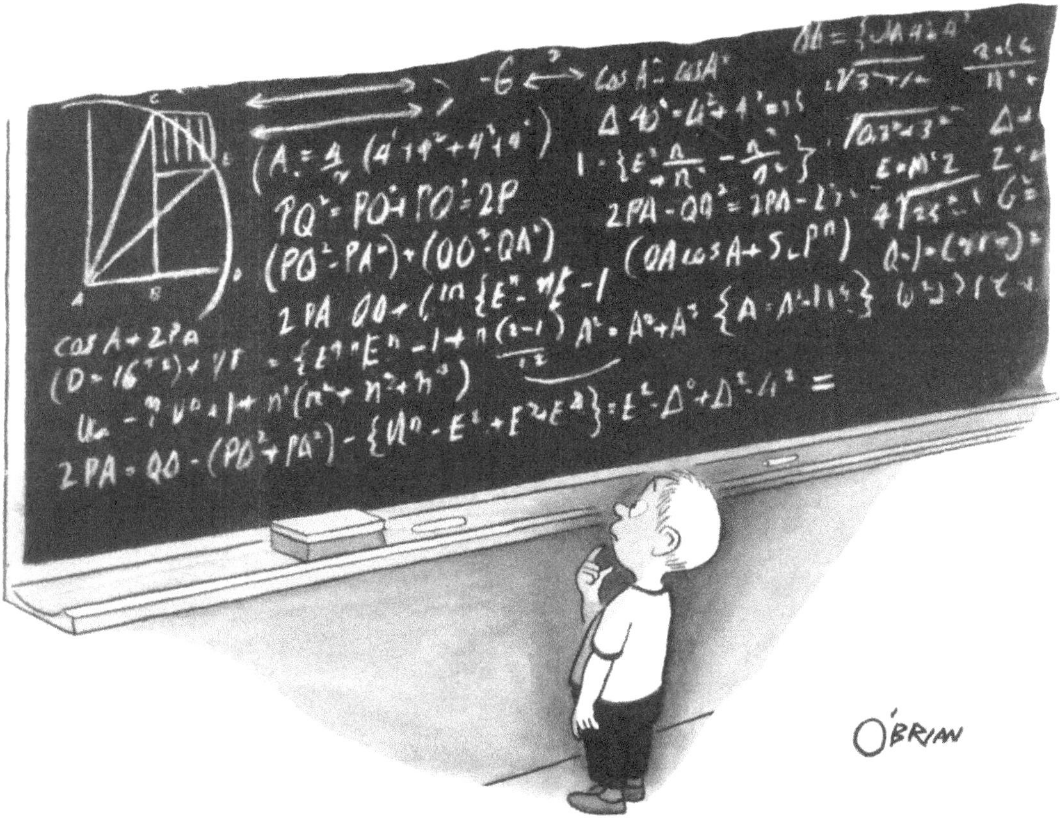
O'BRIAN

"Think!"

"If I may, Mr. Perlmutter, I'd like to answer your question with a question."

"But, sweetie, children are the backbone of our educational system."

"Sarah's grades are excellent. She got A+ in 'Yogi Berra: Philosopher or Fall Guy?,' A in 'Dollars and Scents: An Analysis of Post-Vietnam Perfume Advertising,' A– in 'The Final Four as Last Judgment: The N.C.A.A. Tournament from a Religious Perspective,' and A in 'The American Garage Sale: Its Origins, Cultural Implications, and Future.'"

"But is showing you this toy and telling about it the whole story?
Let's take a look at its sales record, as illustrated by this chart,
which compares it with other toys in its price class."

It's Academic
1965:
What is the capital of Idaho?
1975:
Where is Idaho?
1985:
Where is the United States?
1995:
Which planet are we on?

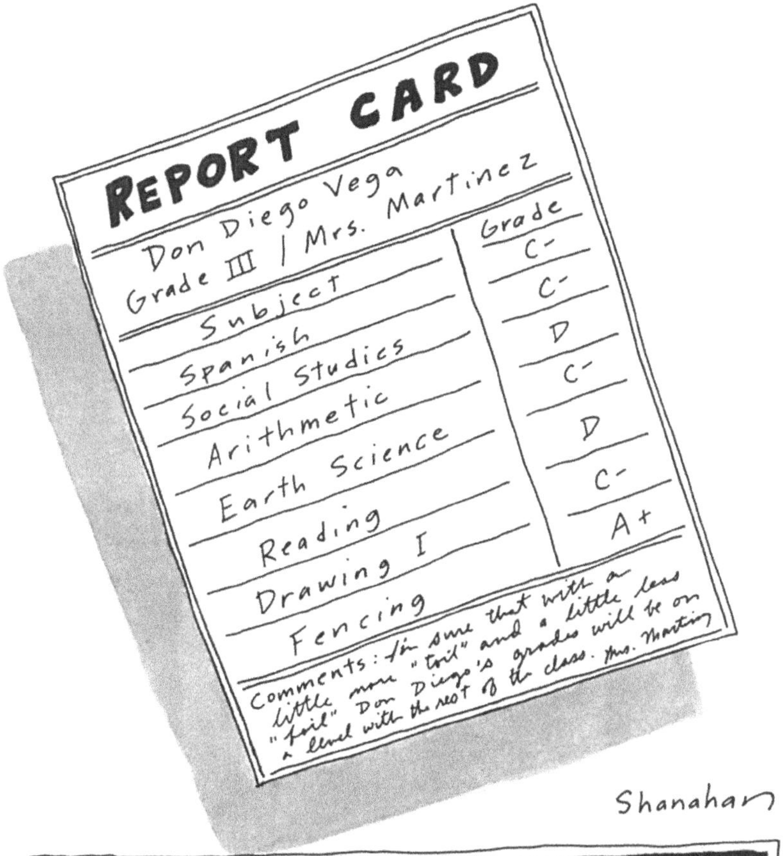
REPORT CARD
Don Diego Vega
Grade III / Mrs. Martinez
Subject
Grade
Spanish C-
Social Studies C-
Arithmetic D
Earth Science C-
Reading D
Drawing I C-
Fencing A+
Comments: I'm sure that with a little more "toil" and a little less "foil" Don Diego's grades will be on a level with the rest of the class. Mrs. Martinez
Shanahan

THE MARKS OF ZORRO

"A note of warning: The following report may contain
material not suitable for the squeamish."

"Miss Jones, may I go home and watch television?"

"You will like Mr. Woofard. He has an attention-deficit disorder."

"We teach them that the world can be an unpredictable, dangerous, and sometimes frightening place, while being careful not to spoil their lovely innocence. It's tricky."

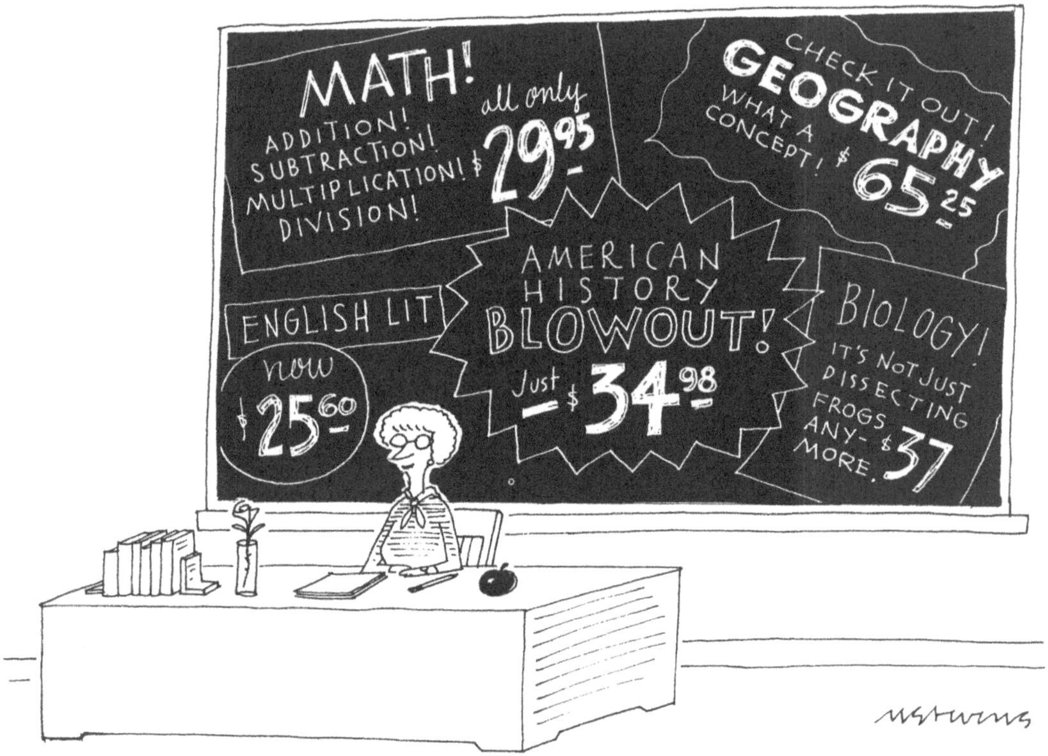
MATH!
ADDITION!
SUBTRACTION!
MULTIPLICATION!
DIVISION!
all only
$29.95
CHECK IT OUT!
GEOGRAPHY
WHAT A CONCEPT!
$65.25
ENGLISH LIT
now
$25.60
AMERICAN HISTORY
BLOWOUT!
Just
$34.98
BIOLOGY!
IT'S NOT JUST DISSECTING FROGS ANY-MORE.
$37

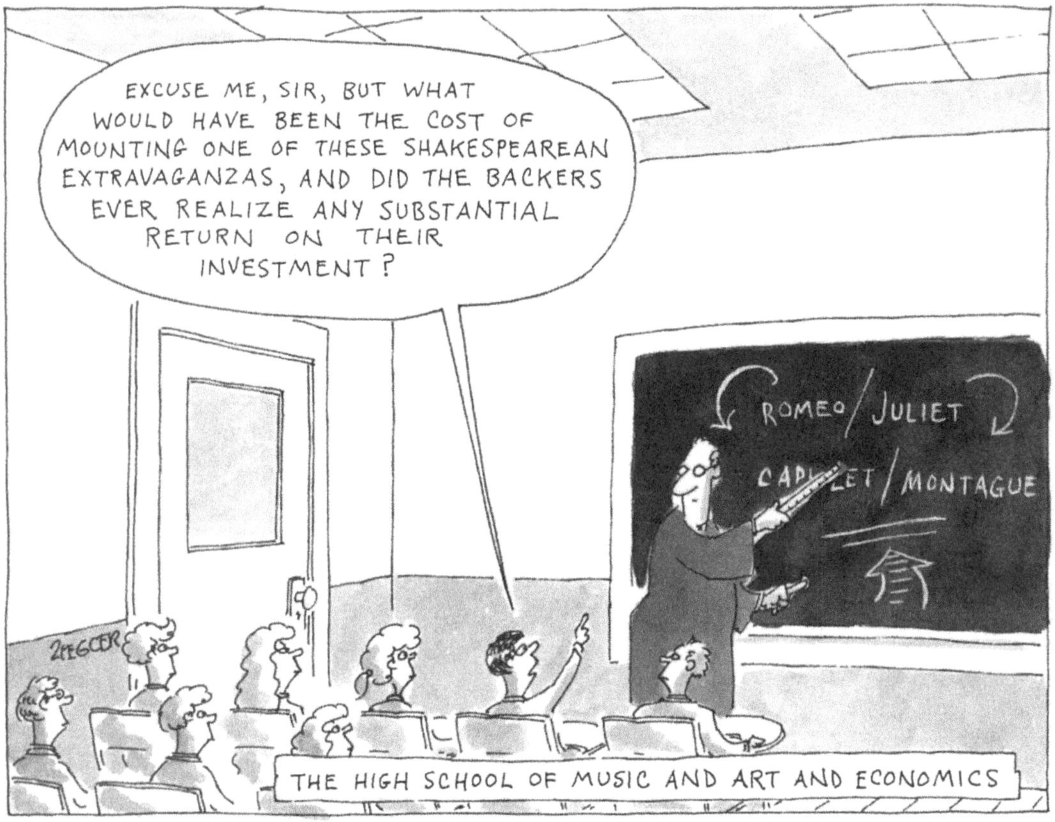
EXCUSE ME, SIR, BUT WHAT WOULD HAVE BEEN THE COST OF MOUNTING ONE OF THESE SHAKESPEAREAN EXTRAVAGANZAS, AND DID THE BACKERS EVER REALIZE ANY SUBSTANTIAL RETURN ON THEIR INVESTMENT?
ROMEO / JULIET
MONTAGUE
THE HIGH SCHOOL OF MUSIC AND ART AND ECONOMICS

"The dog ate my homework."

"'Give me liberty or give me death.' Now, what kind of person
would say something like that?"

"My name is Mr. Collins. I'll be teaching you English literature, and I'm armed."

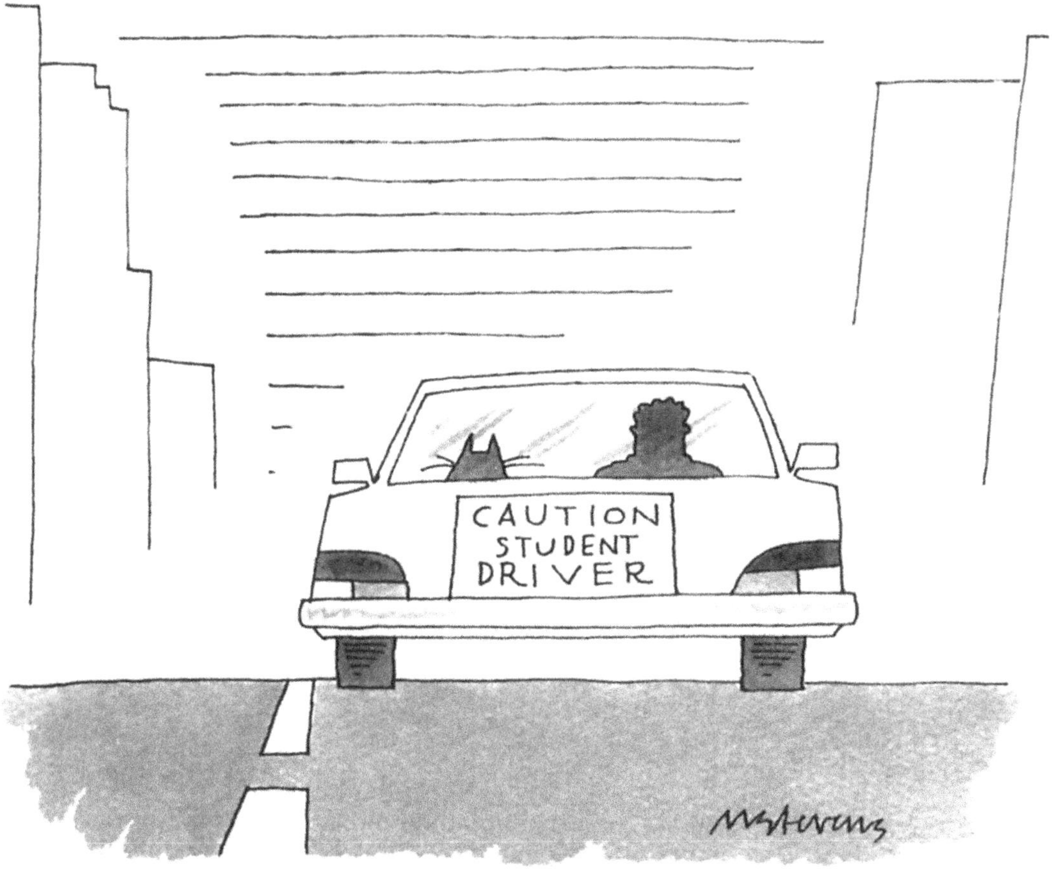
CAUTION
STUDENT
DRIVER
MStevens

"Oh, yes, indeed. We all keep a sharp eye out for those little
clues that seem to whisper 'law' or 'medicine.'"

"I'm sorry, Mr. Landis, would you repeat the question? I was lost in prayer."

"Now you're probably all asking yourselves, 'Why must I learn to read and write?'"

"Today we're going to learn how to deal with rejection."

"I don't have an answer, but you've sure given me a lot to think about."

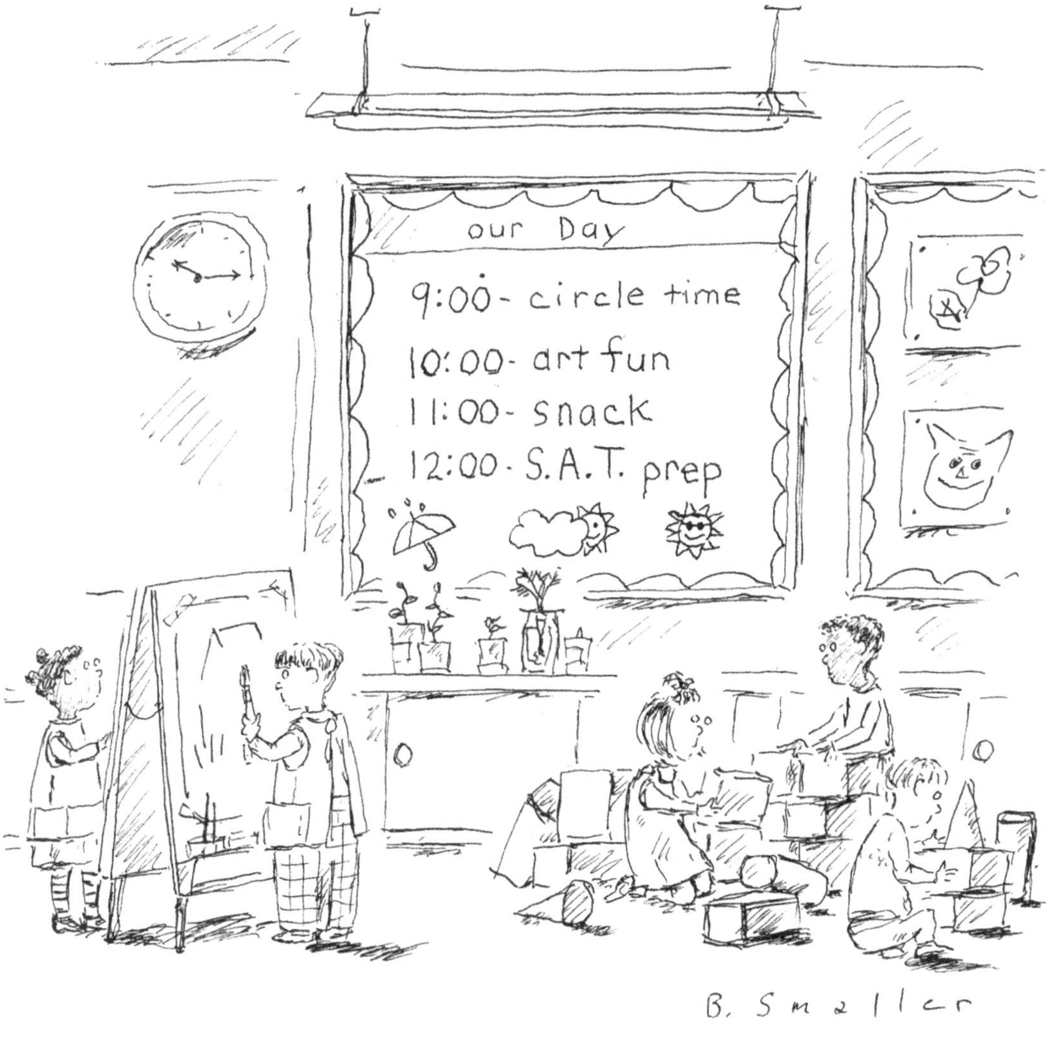
our Day
9:00 - circle time
10:00 - art fun
11:00 - snack
12:00 - S.A.T. prep
B. Smaller

"Jason is cute as a bug, but he sure is one thickheaded little sucker."

"I hope you realize that I'm the one who has to write about this stupid vacation next fall."

"Big deal, an A in math. That would be a D in any other country."

"A lot of homework?"

DECONSTRUCTING LUNCH

① IT'S A SANDWICH:
That, in itself, means you are a _normal_ child from a _normal_ family.

② IT'S ON WHOLE-WHEAT BREAD:
O.K., so we're liberal, big-city Democrats.

③ BUT IT'S THE BIG-BRAND, EASY-TO-CHEW KIND:
I didn't say "radical." I said "liberal."

④ BOLOGNA AND MAYO:
People _always_ mistake us for Republicans!

⑤ IT'S KOSHER BOLOGNA:
It's not about religion—it's about _taste_.

⑥ LETTUCE:
Other parents may not care about their kids' health, but I do.

⑦ LOOK, THERE'S A SLICE OF AMERICAN CHEESE IN THERE:
If you want to become a Mormon, I'll love you anyway. I just want you to be happy.

R. Chast

"And if you'd like your artwork displayed please include a brief bio."

"Those D's are misleading."

"*This is humiliating. Couldn't you drop me a block from school?*"

"Derek's sneakers were made in Malaysia. Can
anyone show us where Malaysia is?"

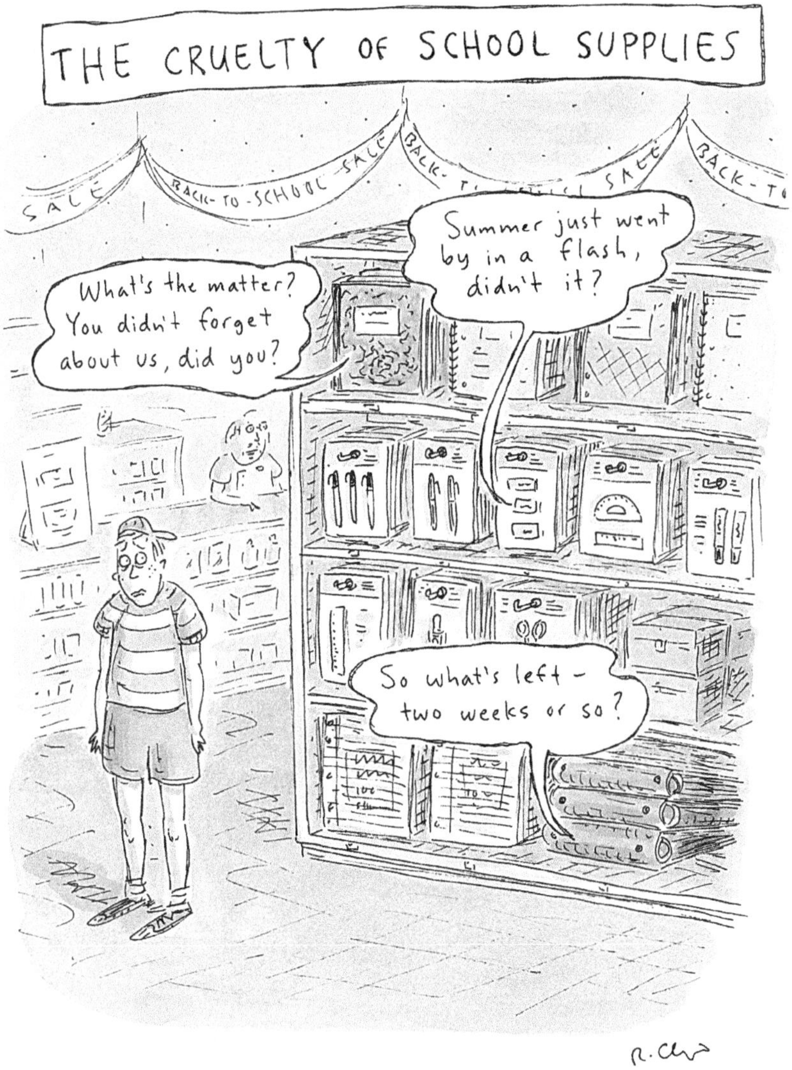
THE CRUELTY OF SCHOOL SUPPLIES
What's the matter? You didn't forget about us, did you?
Summer just went by in a flash, didn't it?
So what's left – two weeks or so?

"I'm sorry, Ms. Greer, but I can't function under this kind of scrutiny."

"Mister Jackson! You know how I feel about sampling."

"Please remind your mom and dad that it's a parent-teacher conference, not a parent-teacher-attorney conference."

SCHOOL CLOSINGS
OF THE FUTURE

September 11-20: BACK-TO-SCHOOL BREATHER
October 11-18: COLUMBUS WEEK
November 1-20: FALL RECESS
November 25-30: THANKSGIVING
December 1-31: CHRISTMAS/HANUKKAH MONTH
January 7-23: WINTER BREAK
All of February: PRESIDENTS' MONTH
March 9-20: PRE-SPRING BREATHER
April 5-30: EASTER VACATION
May 11-23: MAY DAYS
June 2: LAST DAY OF SCHOOL

"You were kept after school to review multiplication and division. This is not a date."

"Here's the deal, Josh—these two gentlemen want to turn
that note you passed in homeroom into a movie."

"If nothing else, school has prepared me for a lifetime of backpacking."

"It's one thing for the National Commission to comment on the quality of teaching in our schools. It's another thing entirely for you to stand up and call Mr. Costello a yo-yo."

"I don't have my homework, Miss Flynn—my parents forgot to do it."

ADMISSIONS TEST
FOR THE
DANBURY INSTITUTE OF PHILOSOPHY

1. How many minutes a day do you spend thinking?
☐ two or fewer ☐ fifteen ☐ a billion

2. Are your thoughts:
☐ like a slow, orderly procession of elephants, or...
☐ like rabbits chasing each other in circles, or...
☐ like gnats?

3. What are your thoughts mostly about?
☐ sex in the year 3000   ☐ parallel parking
☐ mealtime   ☐ illness and death
☐ getting back at people ☐ real estate

4. Which outward signs usually accompany your thinking (check any that apply)?
☐ wrinkled forehead   ☐ index finger pointing to temple
☐ tongue protruding from mouth ☐ hair standing on end

MAIL COMPLETED FORM TO:
Plato Jones
Suite 410
Danbury Industrial Tower and Rotunda
Danbury, New York

"Maybe it's not a wrong answer—maybe it's just a different answer."

"*What I Did on My Summer Vacation: A Mystical Journey of Sexual Awakening.*"

"Your daughter is a pain in the ass."

"O.K., Willy, drag yourself to the table and collapse in despair. Enter Biff."

"When people say 'Do the math,' is this the kind of thing they're referring to?"

"'Giant Sequoias'—with apologies to the Encyclopaedia Britannica."

"This is where I come to unwind."

"'No More School: A Dream Unfulfilled,' by Howard Willocoski."

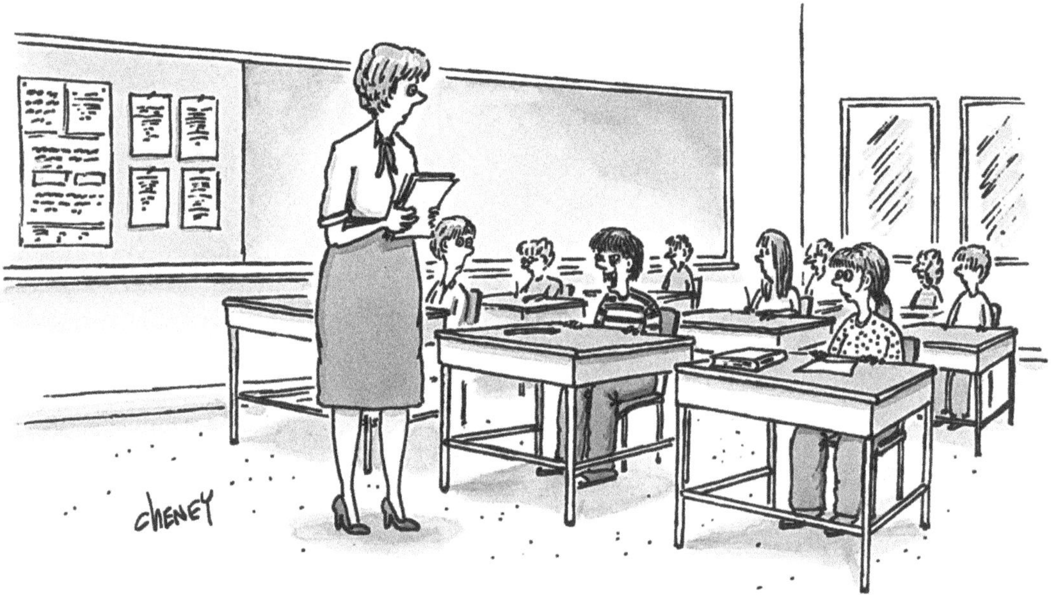
CHENEY

"I ate my homework."

"What does he know, and how long will he know it?"

"*Keep your eyes on your own screen.*"

"She's utterly lacking in group integration."

"I'm taking my voucher and going to circus school."

"Being a scientist is going to be a lot easier than I thought."

"Before I read about my summer vacation, I'd like to ask that all pagers, beepers, and cell phones be turned off."

"Today we're going to explore in paint how we feel
when we're picked up late from preschool."

"The title of my science project is 'My Little Brother: Nature or Nurture.'"

"The innocence seems forced."

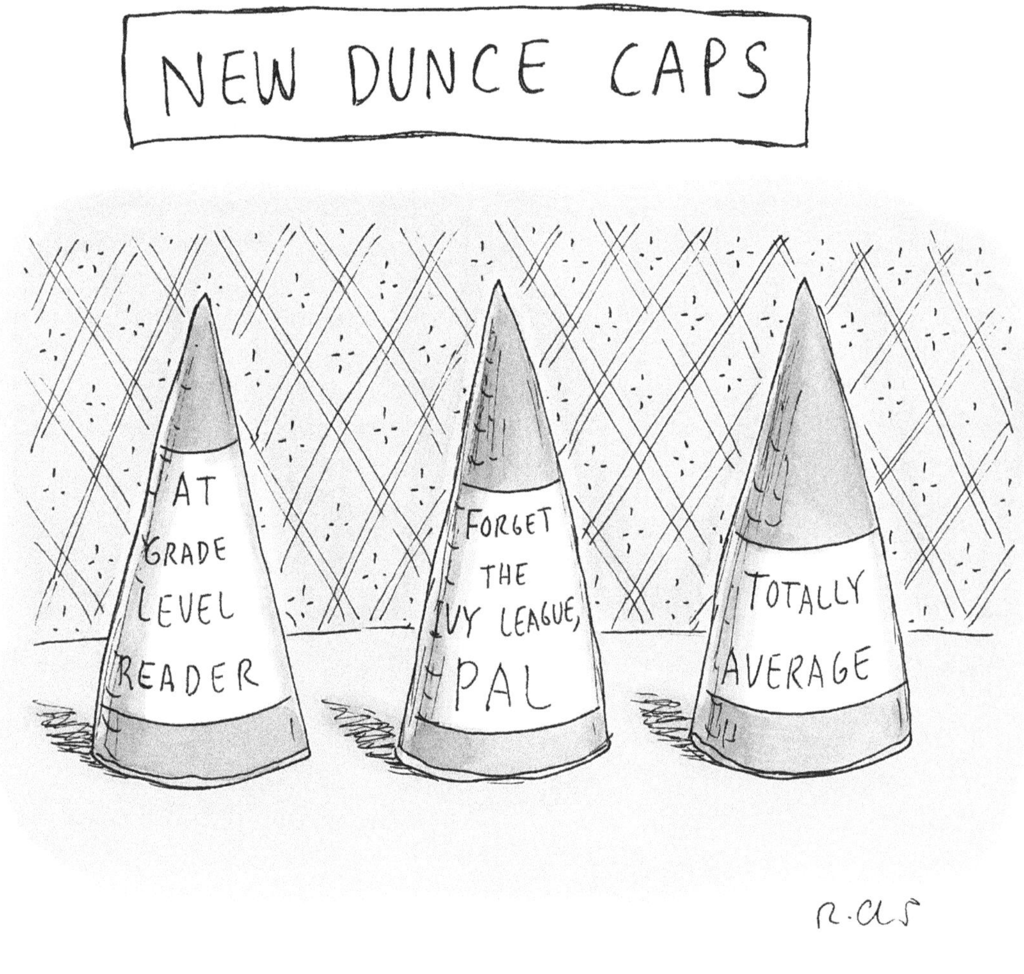
NEW DUNCE CAPS
AT GRADE LEVEL READER
FORGET THE IVY LEAGUE, PAL
TOTALLY AVERAGE

"I'm the only survivor from last semester—what do I win?"

"It may be wrong, but it's how I feel."

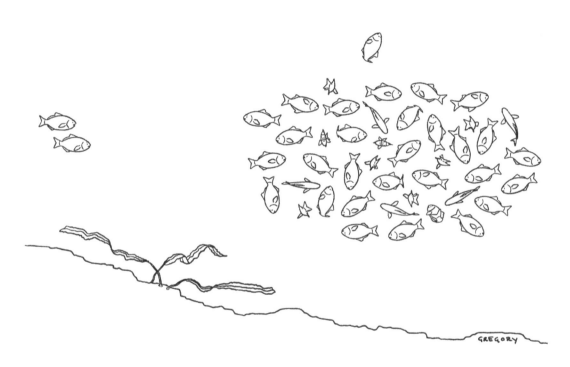

"I believe that's a Montessori school."

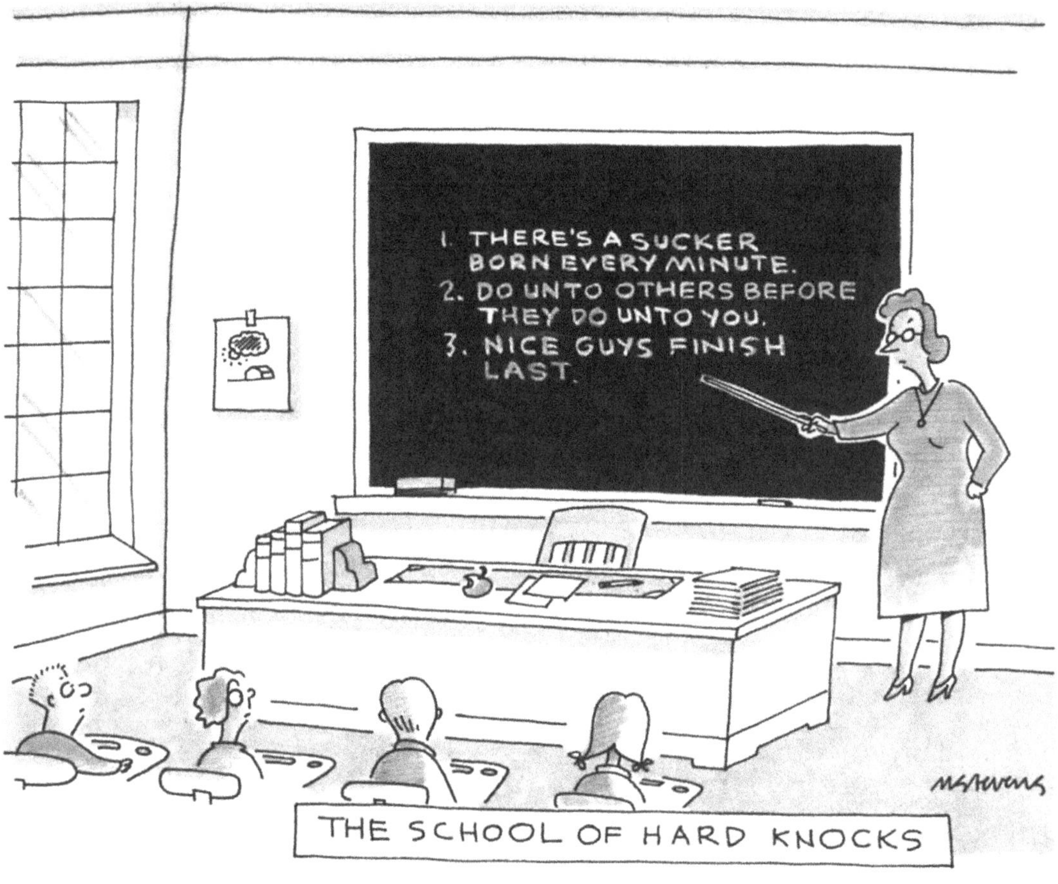
1. THERE'S A SUCKER BORN EVERY MINUTE.
2. DO UNTO OTHERS BEFORE THEY DO UNTO YOU.
3. NICE GUYS FINISH LAST.
THE SCHOOL OF HARD KNOCKS

"If I had _my_ way we wouldn't let _any_ kids in!"

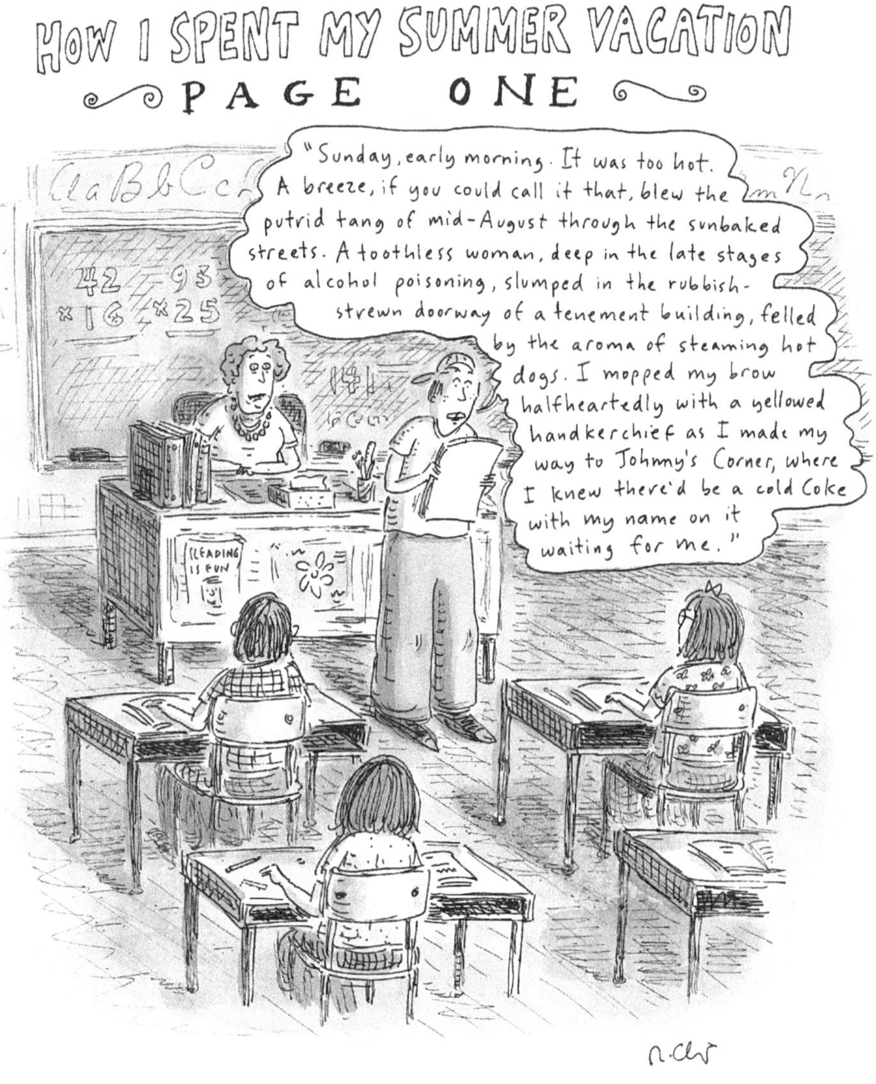
HOW I SPENT MY SUMMER VACATION
PAGE ONE
"Sunday, early morning. It was too hot. A breeze, if you could call it that, blew the putrid tang of mid-August through the sunbaked streets. A toothless woman, deep in the late stages of alcohol poisoning, slumped in the rubbish-strewn doorway of a tenement building, felled by the aroma of steaming hot dogs. I mopped my brow halfheartedly with a yellowed handkerchief as I made my way to Johnny's Corner, where I knew there'd be a cold Coke with my name on it waiting for me."

"I thought it was pretty good, for a book."

"*I pledged allegiance yesterday.*"

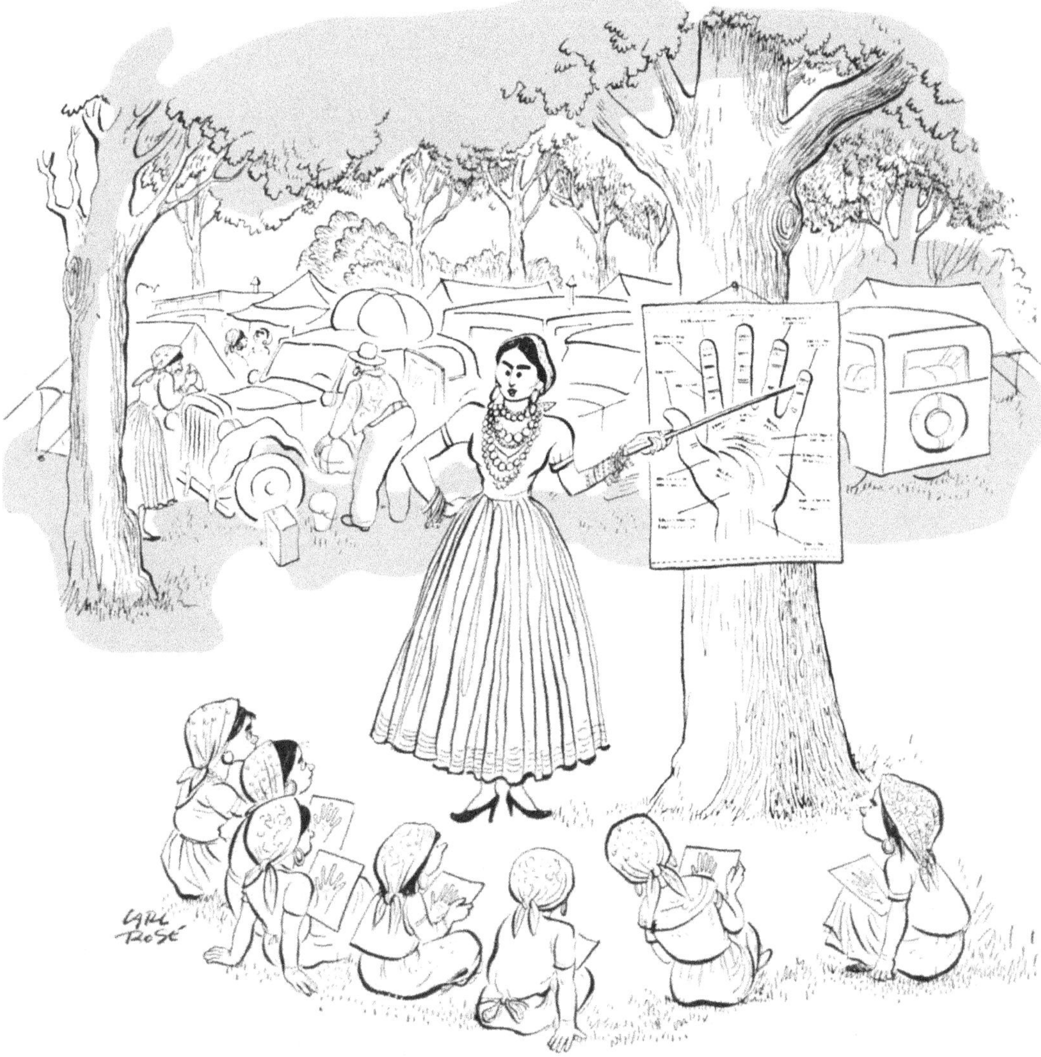
CARL ROSE

"And that's how ya clean a deer!"

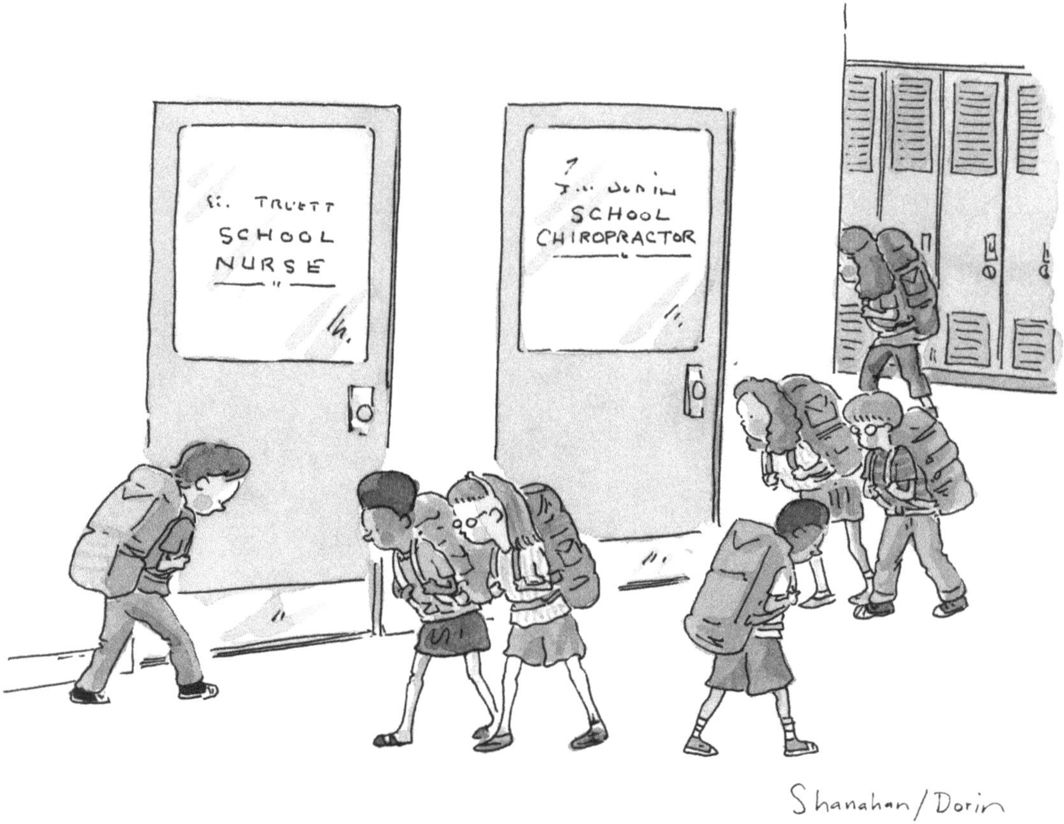
SCHOOL
NURSE
SCHOOL
CHIROPRACTOR
Shanahan/Dorin

"My composition is called 'Mrs. Torrence Is a Big Fat Idiot.'"

"Do you get overtime for this, Miss Marble?"

"Well, it was sort of like a cook-out."

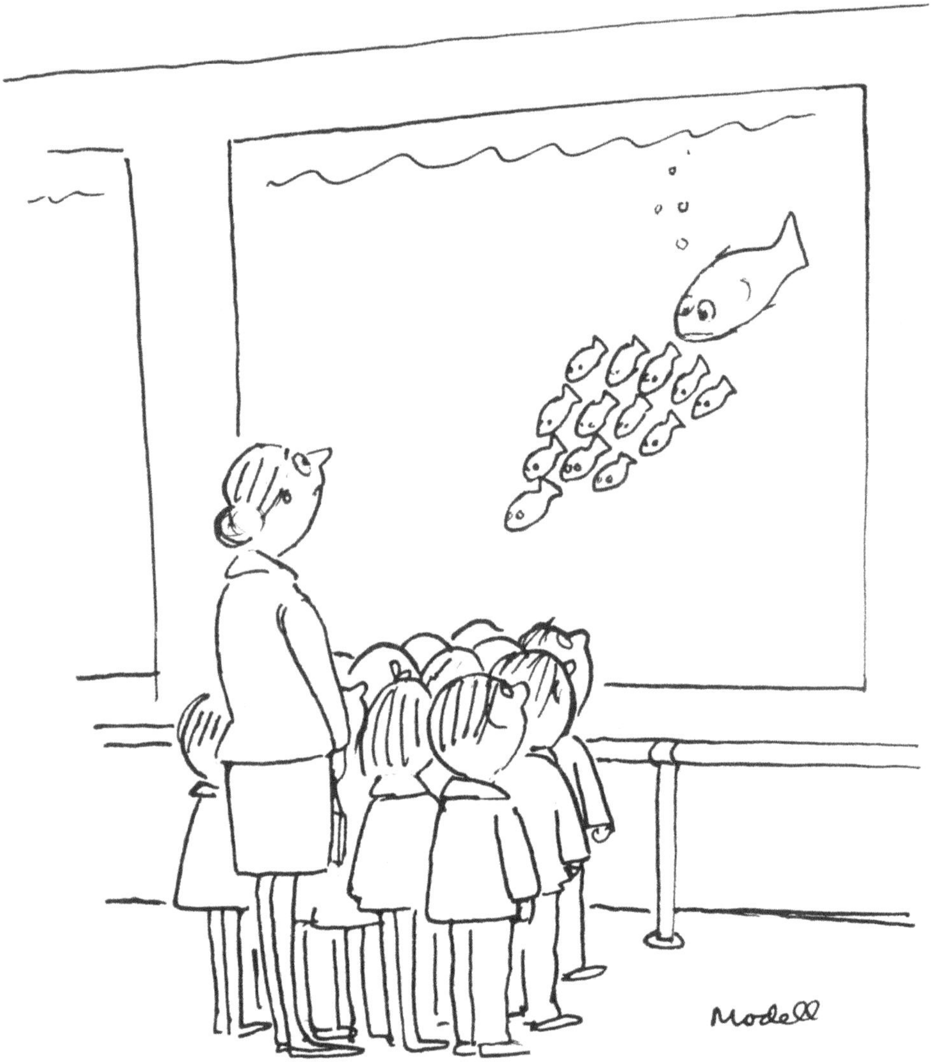
Modell

"The first one to fall asleep gets today's competitive-edge award."

"And another way to help the economy would be to boost teachers' salaries."

"Today's lecture is on loyalty."

THE KNOWLEDGE HUT ®

FORMERLY P.S. 102

INDEX OF ARTISTS